weblinks

You don't need a computer to use this book. But, for readers who do have access to the Internet, the book provides links to recommended websites which offer additional information and resources on the subject.

You will find weblinks boxes like this on some pages of the book.

weblinks

For more information about caring for your pet, go to www.waylinks.co.uk/ series/soyouwant/animals

waylinks.co.uk

To help you find the recommended websites easily and quickly, weblinks are provided on our own website, **waylinks.co.uk.** These take you straight to the relevant websites and save you typing in the Internet address yourself.

Internet safety

↗ Never give out personal details, which include: your name, address, school, telephone number, email address, password and mobile number.

↗ Do not respond to messages which make you feel uncomfortable – tell an adult.

↗ Do not arrange to meet in person someone you have met on the Internet.

↗ Never send your picture or anything else to an online friend without a parent's or teacher's permission.

↗ If you see anything that worries you, tell an adult.

A note to adults
Internet use by children should be supervised. We recommend that you install filtering software which blocks unsuitable material.

Website content

The weblinks for this book are checked and updated regularly. However, because of the nature of the Internet, the content of a website may change at any time, or a website may close down without notice. While the Publishers regret any inconvenience this may cause readers, they cannot be responsible for the content of any website other than their own.

HODDER
Wayland

So You Want To Work With

Animals?

Margaret McAlpine

HODDER
Wayland

an imprint of Hodder Children's Books

First published in 2004 by Hodder Wayland,
an imprint of Hodder Children's Books

© Hodder Wayland 2003

Editor: Laura Milne
Inside design: Peta Morey
Cover design: Hodder Wayland

British Library Cataloguing Publication Data
McAlpine, Margaret
So you want to work with animals?
1.Animal specialists - Vocational guidance - Juvenile literature
I.Title
590.2'3

ISBN 0 7502 4456 9

Printed in China by WKT Company Ltd.

Hodder Children's Books
A division of Hodder Headline Limited
338 Euston Road, London NW1 3BH

Picture Acknowledgements. The publishers would like to thank the following
for allowing their pictures to be reproduced in this publication:
Paul Almasy/Corbis 59b; Tony Arruza/Corbis 24, 25; Yann Arthus-Bertrand/
Corbis 13; Patrick Bennett/Corbis 53; Niall Benvie/Corbis 16; Doug Berry/
Corbis 30; Jonathan Blair/Corbis 22; Corbis 15, 20, 40, 51 (both); Jerry Dawes/
RSPCA Photo Library 19b; Dex Images/Corbis 49; Robert Dowling/Corbis 5;
Andrew Forsyth/RSPCA Photo Library 11b, 54; Raymond Gehman/Corbis 38;
Lynn Goldsmith/Corbis 43t; Charles Gupton/Corbis 44; Brownie Harris/Corbis
21; Ralf-Finn Hestoft/Corbis Saba 6; Dave G. Houser/Corbis 59t; Jose Luis
Pelaez, Inc./Corbis 11t; Kelly-Mooney Photography/Corbis 27b; Layne
Kennedy/Corbis 39; Kit Houghton Photography/Corbis 32, 33, 35t, 35b; Earl
& Nazima Kowall/Corbis 7; Robert Maass/Corbis 36; Stephanie Maze/Corbis
56; Gail Mooney/Corbis 52; Richard T. Nowitz/Corbis 19t; John Periam,
Cordaiy Photo Library Ltd./Corbis 41, 46; Steve Prezant/Corbis 8; Michael
Prince/Corbis 27t; Jeffrey L. Rotman/Corbis 47; Jeffrey Allan Salter/Corbis Saba
37; Kevin Schafer/Corbis 55; Michael St. Maur Sheil/Corbis 28; Ariel
Skelley/Corbis 9, 17; Monika Smith, Cordaiy Photo Library Ltd./Corbis 45;
Paul A. Souders/Corbis 4, 12, 57; Dale C. Spartas/Corbis 14; Andres Stapff/
Reuters/popperfoto.com 29; Peter Steiner/Corbis 43b; Tom Stewart/Corbis 48;
Nik Wheeler/Corbis 23; Michael S. Yamashita/Corbis 31.

Note: Photographs illustrating the 'day in the life of' pages are posed
by models.

Contents

Words in **bold** can be found in the glossary.

Animal Groomer

What is an animal groomer?

Animal groomers are also known as **animal beauticians**. They make sure pets look their best and are in good condition. Animal groomers bath and shampoo animals. They dry them, brush or comb them to get rid of tangles and then clip and trim their coats. Sometimes they might 'finish' an animal with some kind of decoration, such as a bow.

Many animal groomers have their own grooming parlours, while some work for other people. Animal groomers will usually visit pets in their home if necessary and also treat dogs in vets' practices.

Lots of different pets, including dogs, cats, rabbits and guinea pigs need regular grooming. This is especially true for long-haired animals such English sheepdogs, Persian cats, angora rabbits, and Peruvian guinea pigs.

For most pets the treatment is part of regular care, to make sure coats don't become matted, dirty or smelly. However, sometimes owners have their pets groomed professionally before entering them in pet shows or competitions.

A bath and shampoo are needed before a haircut.

Health and beauty

Groomers not only make pets look good, they make them feel good as well. Some animals, especially those with long hair, need to pay a visit to a groomer every month or six weeks. For others a shampoo and trim once a year is enough.

When preparing animals for shows or competitions, groomers need to know exactly what the judges will be looking for in a particular breed, as each breed has **breed standards**. For example, this could be a certain length of ear and size of head.

Knowing the breed standard is important as the animal groomer can then trim and style the coat of the animal to make sure it looks its best. A small number of groomers specialize in caring for dogs of a particular breed.

weblinks

For more information about dog breeds, go to www.waylinks.co.uk/ series/soyouwant/animals

Main tasks of an animal groomer

The main tasks of an animal groomer include:

Bathing and shampooing
Animals with short hair can often lick themselves clean, but others with long or thick curly hair need help. Groomers have a range of animal shampoos and conditioners from which to choose, including beauty products for that extra silky coat.

Brushing and combing
Careful brushing and combing gets rid of knots in the hair and also any fluff or twigs that have become attached to the animal. Groomers usually work with the animal on a **grooming table**, so they can reach every part of its body.

Clipping dogs takes time and patience.

Clipping
Groomers use different equipment including scissors, razors and electrical clippers.

Good points and bad points

'I love treating an animal in bad condition and seeing it leave looking good.'

'Sometimes an animal has to be **sedated** by a vet, before I can groom it. This means giving it an injection to send it to sleep, so it will keep still while I do my work. I find this quite distressing.'

A lot of care is needed, especially when trimming areas around the face and eyes and the legs and paws. Sometimes the animal's head is put through a **restraint** before the clipping starts. This does not hurt the animal, but helps to keep it still during grooming.

All pets, no matter how small, need regular grooming.

Pets sometimes need extra personal care, which an animal groomer can provide. For example:

- Claws or nails of domestic pets often grow too long, and if left they can grow into the soft footpad and cause infection. To avoid this, regular trimming is needed.
- Ears need to be kept clean and the hair inside them trimmed, to stop tiny creatures called **mites** collecting there and causing sores.
- Teeth need **scaling** and cleaning in the same way as human teeth, to avoid decay and gum problems.
- **Parasites** are fleas and other tiny creatures that feed off the blood of other animals and live in their hair or fur. These cause sores and irritation and even skin infections if they are not removed, using special powders, lotions or shampoos.

Skills needed to be an animal groomer

Confidence
Animal groomers need to be calm and confident as animals can tell very quickly when humans are nervous. They need to handle animals confidently and firmly, which can be difficult when animals struggle.

Communication
Good communication skills are important in this job, as animal groomers need to explain clearly to owners what treatments are needed and why. They also need to be tactful and sometimes tell owners politely that they are not looking after their pets properly.

Strength and stamina
Animal groomers need to be physically strong because some animals such as large dogs take a lot of strength to hold and control. Also they have to stand on their feet all day.

A steady hand is needed for the job.

Dexterity
It is important to be good with your hands in this job, as a single slip with a clipper or scissors can hurt an animal badly.

Awareness of health and safety
Grooming parlours need to be kept very clean, and equipment such as scissors and clippers must be sterilised every time they are used. Otherwise, parasites and infections could spread from one animal to another.

Groomers advise owners on how to care for their pets at home.

Artistic skill

It takes a good eye to make an animal look its best.

Business skills

Many animal groomers are **self-employed**, running their own business. Good business skills such as **bookkeeping**, managing money and being well organised in keeping notes and records are therefore vital to the success of the job.

fact file

There are three main ways to train as an animal groomer:

• By paying for a training course in animal grooming at a private centre or college.

• By learning on the job – training for a National Vocational Qualification while working with an experienced groomer.

• By gaining a training place as a **Modern Apprentice**.

A day in the life of an animal groomer

Sue Evans

Sue has been an animal groomer for many years and runs her own grooming parlour.

8.00 am The day starts and owners arrive with their pets. Some of them prefer to wait, while others drop their pets off and call back for them later.

8.30 am Time to tackle a regular visitor, a sheepdog, which comes in every few weeks for a shampoo and trim. He's used to me and lets me clean his teeth as well. You can only do this if you start when animals are very young and win their trust, otherwise they have to be **anaesthetised**.

9.45 am My next patient is a long-haired rabbit, which needs careful grooming and clipping.

12.30 pm I nip into my car and drive to the home of a budgerigar to clip its beak and claws. It's easier to clip birds in their own surroundings, than have them brought to the parlour.

2.00 pm Back at the parlour, there's time for a quick lunch.

2.30 pm My next case is a pet cat in a sad state, with matted fur and a lot of fleas. It's badly in need of grooming. There's nothing to be done except to give it a very short haircut and treat its infected bites. I then have a word with its owner about caring for the coat when it grows again.

Often owners don't realise that all animals have fleas, and regular treatment is needed to stop them making life miserable for their pet.

3.30 pm   I'm off to a local vet who has asked me to groom a dog. The animal is so nervous it needs an **anaesthetic** before it can be treated.

4.15 pm   Back to the parlour to check for messages and make a few phone calls before signing off for the day.

Owners phone up to book their pets in for a grooming session.

High standards of cleanliness are vital in a grooming parlour.

weblinks

For more information about caring for your pet, go to www.waylinks.co.uk/ series/soyouwant/animals

Animal Shelter Worker

What is an animal shelter worker?

Animal shelter workers work in animal shelters, which provide homes for pets whose owners can no longer look after them and for wild animals recovering from injury. With wild animals the aim is to release them back into the wild as soon as possible; with tame animals it is to find them new owners.

Workers care for different types of animals, including:

- dogs;
- cats;
- large field animals such as horses and ponies;
- rabbits;
- small animals such as guinea pigs, gerbils, rats and mice.

Some shelters look after all sorts of different animals, whereas others specialize in one type of animal such as horses or donkeys.

Sometimes animals are brought in as strays or because they have been neglected or cruelly treated, but most come from good homes and had caring owners, who became unable to care for them. For example, an elderly dog owner might need to move into a retirement home where

A wake-up call for the animals and time to check they are all in good spirits.

Return to the wild

Injured wild animals are often brought into shelters by members of the public. Treating wild animals is not easy. They are not used to any sort of human contact and often need to be **sedated** before they can be examined or treated.

Wild animals do not make good pets and it is cruel to try and keep them in captivity. They need to return to the wild as soon as possible, while they can remember how to hunt for food and defend themselves against other animals.

Most shelters have special units for mothers and babies.

pets are not allowed. A family could move from the country to a city where there is no space for a pony. A child might develop an **allergy** to animal fur, so the family can no longer keep their cat or dog.

Most animal shelters try to **rehome** animals as quickly as possible, moving them on after just a few weeks. If an animal has problems such as fear of humans, it might stay longer and elderly horses or donkeys may retire to a shelter for the rest of their lives.

weblinks

For more information on rehoming animals, go to www.waylinks.co.uk/ series/soyouwant/animals

Main tasks of an animal shelter worker

Usually shelter workers work with one type of animal such as cats. Their job includes:

- feeding and checking for any health or behaviour problems;
- cleaning out pens and kennels and changing bedding;
- looking after animals which are ill or have had medical treatment or operations;
- grooming animals;
- exercising animals such as dogs and horses;
- playing with animals, helping them to grow used to people;
- showing visitors around and talking to them about the animals.

Training animals to improve their behaviour is important if they are to be re-homed.

Good points and bad points

'I feel I can make a difference, working with a stray cat – seeing it begin to look better and helping it to become more sociable. The worst part of the job is when an animal has to be put down because it is ill or in pain.'

Most shelters welcome visitors every day.

Some animals are in a shelter because of their behaviour. A dog may bark all night and disturb the neighbours, or snap at people and frighten them. A cat may refuse to use its **litter tray** and soil around the house.

In the past, animals with behaviour problems were unsuitable for rehoming. These animals would either stay in the shelter for a long time or have to be put down. Today the aim is to change bad behaviour. Shelters often employ **animal behaviourists** to teach animals good habits. Animal shelter workers are involved in this work, doing exercises with the animals and treating them in ways suggested by the behaviourist.

The public are encouraged to visit animal shelters. Many shelters are charities which means they need money from supporters to keep up the good work. Animal shelter workers welcome visitors and talk to them about the animals. The hope is that those visitors who do not want a pet will donate money for the shelter's upkeep.

Skills needed to be an animal shelter worker

Realism

Although animal shelter workers need to love animals and enjoy being with them, they also have to be realistic about the job. Animals are not just sweet fluffy creatures, to cuddle and play with. They can be difficult and bad tempered and take a lot of looking after. Animal shelter workers also need to accept that sometimes animals have to be **put down**.

Unsqueamish

Some animals that arrive in shelters are badly trained, **maltreated**, or very ill. Animal shelter workers must be able to cope with smells, mess and dirt and have strong stomachs to clean up after the animals.

Knowledge of health and safety

Shelters must be very clean, to avoid animals infecting each other with illnesses and parasites. Workers need to understand why cleanliness is necessary and keep runs, shelters and feeding equipment scrubbed and disinfected.

Knowledge of nutrition

Animal shelter workers must have a knowledge of animal nutrition to be able to look after baby animals, those which are sick or old, and those which need special diets.

Animal shelter staff work to give the animals the best help possible.

First aid

Although animal shelters have regular visits from vets, shelter workers need to be able to give first aid to animals that suddenly become ill or are injured.

Animals needing care come in all shapes and sizes.

Patience
Patience is important because it takes time and effort to deal with nervous, worried animals.

Teamwork
Animal shelter workers have to work as part of a team, together with other shelter workers, veterinary nurses, animal behaviourists and vets.

Communication
Dealing with a lot of outside visitors means that workers must be polite, friendly and sociable. They also have to explain facts clearly and simply to visitors who have a lot of questions.

fact file

There are no formal qualifications needed to be an animal shelter worker. Many people want to work with animals, and when jobs are advertised there are often lots of applicants. Shelters are looking for people with experience of working with animals. Because the job involves such a lot of contact with the public, they also want staff to have experience of working with the public.

A day in the life of an animal shelter worker

David Roseblade

David has worked in a cat shelter for four years. He has three cats of his own, all from the shelter.

8.00 am	The shelter has a **holding unit** for new arrivals, four **homing units** for cats ready for new homes, an **isolation unit** for sick cats and a mum and kitten unit.
	I make sure the cats in my unit are bright and happy. They are usually housed singly, but sometimes in pairs, or groups of three.
8.15 am	I check in the notebook what each cat is to eat and make breakfast. I have to make sure that each cat fed in a group gets its fair share.
9.00 am	Each individual unit has outside and inside sections which need to be cleaned daily. Cats are clean animals but there's always one that drags its bedding into its water container!
	We take cats needing operations for surgery. Many cats need dental work and all animals are **neutered** before being rehomed.
10.00 am	Visitors arrive looking for a new pet. They give their details including the sort of animal they want. Then they look around and ask us questions.
11.00 am	There are new cats to settle in and others to move on.

12.00 pm	I feed the animals on special diets. Most cats are fed twice a day, but kittens and sick cats need extra feeds.
1.30 pm	I check the newcomers and groom those with tangled fur. Cats need human contact if they are going to be rehomed with families. Some love to play while others are shy and nervous.
3.00 pm	Animals recovering from operations are brought back to the unit.
4.00 pm	A final meal before bedtime and lights out.
4.30 pm	We hand over to security staff.

Seeing pets leave to go to a caring new owner is one of the best parts of the job.

Animal quarters have to be cleaned every day.

weblinks

For more information on the work of an animal shelter, go to www.waylinks.co.uk/ series/soyouwant/animals

Marine Biologist

What is a marine biologist?

Marine biologists study the oceans and seas, beaches and coastlines, and the animal and plant life in and on them. The animals they study include:

- whales, dolphins and porpoises (known as cetaceans);
- **marine mammals** such as seals and sea lions;
- marine birds;
- fish;
- **invertebrates** (animals without back bones such as shellfish and crabs).

Marine biologists carry out research into different aspects of sea life. This could mean looking at one particular species, or examining all the marine life in a particular ocean area, or considering changes in a stretch of coastline.

Films and television programmes showing marine biologists swimming with dolphins and working with whales and sharks, have made marine biology seem very glamorous. However, this sort of work is only one small area of

There is still a great deal to be discovered about marine life.

The earth's oceans

71% of the earth's surface is covered by oceans. Over 200,000 different animals and plants live in the sea. Materials from marine plants are used in the manufacture of many goods including toothpaste and ice cream.

The work of marine biologists is vital for the future of the earth.

Some marine biologists spend all their time in laboratories.

marine biology and it is also the most difficult to get into. Other work includes working in laboratories and writing up reports. So, although marine biology is a very interesting subject, it is sometimes not as exciting as it appears to be on the screen.

Some marine biologists teach in colleges and universities, or work for governments or private companies doing research into marine life. Others work on fish farms or in **aquariums**, or on **research ships**.

weblinks

For more information on the world's oceans and life in them, go to www.waylinks.co.uk/ series/soyouwant/animals

Main tasks of a marine biologist

Marine biology is not just one particular job. It can be divided into different areas of study. These are:

- Biodiversity – the study of different types of life in the same area of water.
- Deep sea biology – the study of life on the seabed.
- Fisheries biology – the study of fish and fishing methods which use boats.
- Aquaculture – the study of fish farming methods where fish and shellfish are bred commercially; to be sold as food.
- Cold marine biology – the study of marine life in cold seas; such as the Arctic Ocean.
- **Temperate** marine biology – the study of marine life in cool seas; such as the Atlantic Ocean.
- Warm marine biology – the study of marine life in warm seas; such as the Indian Ocean.
- Coastal biology – the study of beaches and areas where the sea meets dry land.

Keeping check of fishing catches is important to make sure that too many fish are not taken from one area.

Good points and bad points

'I love the freedom of being in the water, swimming with the animals.'

'The part of my job that I don't enjoy so much is sitting behind a desk coping with the paperwork.'

Some marine biologists have diving qualifications and go on diving expeditions to photograph plants and animals, or to find specimens, which they take away to examine. Some spend a lot of time in the open air, examining beaches, rock pools and **estuaries**, while others work indoors in laboratories or on board **research ships**.

Humans rely on the world's oceans for fish, shellfish and extracts from marine plants, but there are many threats to oceans from human behaviour, for example:

- waste materials are dumped into the sea causing pollution;
- large areas are fished so heavily that certain types of fish are in danger of extinction.

Marine biologists study the effects that these threats are having on the oceans' **ecosystems**. The future health of the planet depends on us having a greater understanding about it and the delicate life systems within it. This is why the work of marine biologists is so important.

Skills needed to be a marine biologist

Scientific
As well as needing to have a strong interest in science and the environment, marine biologists must have a scientific background and a degree in marine biology.

Determination
It takes at least four or five years of studying to gain the qualifications needed and then, because it is a popular career choice and lots of people would like to be marine biologists, finding work is not always easy.

Adventurous
A lot of marine biologists have to travel wherever there is work. In some cases this could mean living abroad for long periods of time.

Communication
Both writing well and speaking well are vital. This is because writing reports about experiments and findings is an important part of the job, as is talking confidently and in an interesting way to other scientists, and to people who have little scientific knowledge.

Gathering specimens to examine in the lab.

Observation
Good observation skills are crucial, as marine biologists have to be able to notice even very small changes taking place over a long time.

Sharing ideas is the way forward.

fact file

To be a marine biologist you need to go to university and take a degree in marine biology or a subject similar to it. This is usually followed by further study and research, such as a PhD qualification.

Teamwork

Marine biologists need to enjoy working as part of a team as they do not usually work alone, but as part of a group with other scientists.

Diving

A lot of marine biologists carry out work in the sea and need to have a diving qualification in order to do this.

A day in the life of a marine biologist

Juan Romero

Juan is a marine biologist and works at a large aquarium.

It's difficult to talk about a typical day because I spend at least a week every month abroad. My next trip is to Dubai to survey the **artificial reef**, built by the Dubai Government. I shall be diving down to collect specimens, check pollution levels and examine the state of the reef itself. I shall also do some underwater filming while I'm there.

I'm involved in a project in Spain, examining fish in the Mediterranean and I also give lectures in different countries. I'm very fortunate to work as a marine biologist, because many people who study the subject are unable to find work in the field and have to take other jobs.

9.00 am   If my day is to be spent at the aquarium, my first job is to check my post and emails.

10.00 am   I spend some time diving into the tanks to observe the fish and check all is well.

A great deal of maintenance work is necessary, cleaning **valves** and **outlets**. One of my major tasks is cleaning the windows, to make sure visitors have a good view into the tanks.

There are around 65 tanks in the aquarium including one which is 11 metres deep. Species include sharks up to 2.5 metres in length, and sea turtles.

12.00 pm   Time for some administration work in the office.

2.00 pm   I lecture in marine biology at the university and the afternoon is spent there, taking classes and discussing work with individual students.

A visit to an aquarium is an opportunity for members of the public to see what life is like under the sea.

Educating people is an important part of a marine biologist's work.

weblinks

For more information on the work of aquariums, go to www.waylinks.co.uk/series/soyouwant/animals

Riding Instructor

What is a riding instructor?

Riding instructors teach people of all ages to ride horses and ponies. Pupils range from young children who ride for fun to serious competition riders. Riding instructors are found in riding schools of all sizes. Some schools are small with just a few horses or ponies, owned by an instructor who works alone. Others are big operations with all-weather facilities such as an indoor riding arena and a large number of staff.

The job of the riding instructor is to make sure riders learn to:

- ride correctly and safely – bad habits such as sitting in the wrong position can cause problems;
- improve the standard of their riding;
- look after both the horse and riding equipment including **saddle**, **bridle** and **head collar**;
- enjoy themselves.

Experienced riding instructors may specialize in training riders for competitions at national

Riding instructors need to love horses.

Danger!

Riding is classed as a high risk sport, second only in danger to motor racing. It takes a great deal of skill and a cool head to ride at speed without putting the animal or the rider in danger.

All riders need to be aware of the need for safety and to wear a hard riding hat at all times.

or international level, such as the Olympic Games. There are several different kinds of competition, including:

- Showjumping – where riders and horses complete a route, jumping over obstacles on the way.
- Dressage – in which animals and riders are judged on the way they stand and the way in which the horse follows commands.
- Eventing – in which horses and riders take part in events which usually last around three days and include cross country riding, showjumping and dressage.
- Endurance – events lasting several days where riders and horses cover long distances.

Many people with physical and mental disabilities enjoy riding.

weblinks

For more information on becoming a riding instructor, go to www.waylinks.co.uk/series/soyouwant/animals

Main tasks of a riding instructor

The first task of a riding instructor is to talk to riders, to judge their ability, and to find out if they have any riding experience. Then a training plan is drawn up for each rider, outlining the level at which they want to ride.

Riding instructors teach riders how to mount a horse, to walk, trot, gallop and jump and how to care for a horse after a ride. They give feedback after a lesson and give demonstrations themselves of riding techniques.

Riders who compete in events and shows need to receive special tuition from instructors. In order to work at national or international competition level, instructors need to be excellent riders themselves and to have a great deal of experience in instruction. They also need to have a good knowledge of competition rules.

It takes a great deal of talent and training to reach top competition level.

Good points and bad points

'Getting up early on a cold, wet winter morning when other people are snug and warm in bed is not much fun. Neither is spending two or three hours in the rain mucking out, feeding and exercising the horses.'

'But helping people to enjoy riding, seeing them improve and become more confident, gives me a lot of pleasure.'

As well as teaching people to ride, instructors also train horses. This is called **breaking in**. It means making sure that a horse is used to someone riding it and obeys commands. It also means working on and improving any weaknesses or bad habits such as head shaking, before the horse is used for riding lessons.

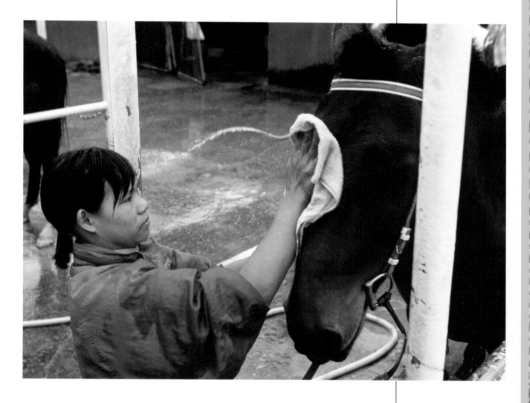

Horse care is also part of a riding instructor's job. Instructors have to get up early to feed, groom and exercise horses and ponies and clean out yards, stables and boxes. Horses are valuable animals and they need a lot of looking after.

An important part of the job is making sure horses are well cared for.

Riding instructors, especially those who are self-employed, need to order feed and equipment and keep business accounts.

Skills needed to be a riding instructor

Physical strength
The work is tough. Riding instructors work long hours, get up early and use a lot of energy on the job. Most of them are outside most of the day, whatever the weather.

Enthusiasm
Riding instructors need to love the job and be able to encourage other people to enjoy riding. They spend all their working day, usually from dawn to dusk, with horses and give up weekends and evenings for their job, so they have to really enjoy it.

Learning to mount a horse properly is one of the first steps.

Patience
To get the best from both horses and riders, a calm, firm approach is needed.
Instructors need to help riders to develop self-confidence and cope with difficulties.

Friendliness
It's important for riders and horses to feel relaxed and comfortable.

Discipline
Riding instructors must be in control of the situation at all times, and, while being pleasant and friendly, they have to make it clear to humans and animals that they are in charge.

Patience is important because riders learn at their own pace.

Teaching skills
Instructors have to give very clear, easily understood instructions to riders and horses. They also have to give good feedback to riders so that they can improve.

Responsible
Riding can be a dangerous activity and riding instructors must have safety in mind at all times.

Riding skills
Instructors need to be excellent riders.

fact file

Riding instructors need a qualification from either the British Horse Society or the Association of British Riding Schools.
These can be gained by:
● becoming a **working pupil** at a riding school;
● taking a full-time college course;
● through distance learning – working to reach the right standard in their own time and then taking the examinations.

A day in the life of a riding instructor

Cindy Russell

Cindy is a riding instructor and an **endurance rider**.

6.30 am   The first job is to check the 23 horses. I work with another instructor and some trainees. We mix feeds for the day, following **diet instructions** for each horse which are written on a blackboard and feed and water the horses.

7.45 am   Time for breakfast – a cup of tea and a piece of toast.

8.00 am   We look at the bookings for the day and decide which riders will ride which horses.

9.00 am   Most of our pupils at this time are groups from local schools. They prepare themselves and their horses for the ride and we set off, either along one of the nearby forest trails, or if the weather is bad, to our outdoor school.

11.00 am   The pupils have gone. The stables and yards have to be mucked out and swept. Horses not used for the lessons have to be exercised and new horses broken in.

1.00 pm   Lunchtime for the horses.

1.30 pm   Lunchtime for the staff.

2.30 pm   I give lessons to the working pupils who are training to be instructors.

4.30 pm   The first afternoon pupils arrive. There are usually eight riders in the group and they are followed an hour later by a second group.

5.30 pm   Time is tight so we use a new set of horses for this group.

7.30 pm   If it's a Tuesday or a Thursday the next two hours are spent teaching adults in the outdoor school. These are serious riders and some of them bring their own horses.

9.30 pm   Time to stable the horses, put in their night hay and switch on the security alarms.

Riding instructors work with advanced riders.

The end of another day.

weblinks

For more information on working with horses, go to www.waylinks.co.uk/ series/soyouwant/animals

Veterinary Surgeon (vet)

What is a vet?

A vet is a person who looks after sick animals, in the same way that a doctor looks after humans. They deal with animals of all sizes and types from pet hamsters to race horses and reptiles.

Most vets work in **private practices**. Sometimes they work alone, but usually they work with a small group of vets. A veterinary practice usually has its own surgery, with waiting rooms, examination rooms, drug store and operating rooms. Owners pay the vet for the treatment given to their pets and for medicines or special food.

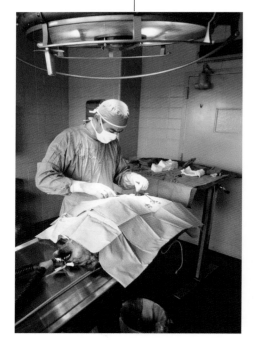

This dog has been given an anaesthetic and is now being operated on by the vet.

Vets give animals an **anaesthetic** to put them to sleep and then carry out routine operations, which have been planned in advance. Animals need an anaesthetic for vets to carry out quite simple jobs like cleaning teeth. Vets also carry out emergency operations on injured animals such as those knocked down in road accidents.

Veterinary practices run an emergency service. This means there is always a vet ready to care for sick animals at weekends and at night. As well as running their own practices, vets often do other work.

A taste for the exotic

Although cats, dogs, fish, hamsters and birds are the most common pets, there is a growing trend for people to keep exotic or unusual animals, such as lizards and snakes. Such pets are delicate and there are vets who specialize in looking after exotic animals.

This vet works for a turtle hospital in Florida, USA.

For example:

● Inspecting farm animals to make sure they are not carrying diseases such as **foot and mouth disease**, which could spread to other farms.
● Checking riding schools, pet shops, catteries and kennels to make sure the animals are well looked after.

Some vets don't work in practices. Instead, they:

● Have jobs in zoos or wildlife parks giving advice on looking after **endangered species** and setting up **breeding programmes**.
● Work in medical **laboratories**, doing research or checking the way animals react to drugs.
● Look after animals for animal welfare organizations such as the RSPCA in the UK, or the ASPCA in the USA.
● Work for the armed forces, looking after their dogs and horses.

Main tasks of a vet

A vet's work includes:

- examining sick animals to find out what is wrong with them;
- treating them with medicines;
- performing operations;
- giving injections to stop animals catching serious illnesses;
- advising owners on how to look after their animals;
- putting sick or unwanted animals to sleep;
- sterilizing animals to stop them reproducing;
- advising farming/governmental bodies on **health programmes**;
- setting standards for animal hygiene, slaughter and meat inspection.

This vet has visited a farm in order to give a pig an injection.

Good points and bad points

'It's a great feeling when I can help a sick animal to recover. When this happens it helps to make up for the times when there's nothing I can do and an animal has to be destroyed.'

'It's never easy telling owners that nothing more can be done for an animal. They are often very distressed because the pet is like a member of their family.'

'Going out on emergency calls is part of the job and it's certainly not good for my social life.'

When animals are old or seriously ill, it is not always possible to cure them. Vets have to explain this to owners and suggest that the best thing to do is to put the animal to sleep painlessly.

In cities vets usually work with pets such as dogs, cats, mice, hamsters, rabbits and caged birds. Their owners bring them to the surgery to see the vet. In country areas, as well as treating household pets, vets also treat farm animals and horses. These animals cannot easily be brought to the surgery, so the vets go out to the animals. This is why vets working in the country need to be able to drive.

This vet specialises in wild animals. Here she is treating a swan.

Skills needed to be a vet

Scientific
Vets must have excellent scientific and biological knowledge. They need to take a veterinary degree and understand **medical terminology**.

Communication
Vets have to be able to explain to owners exactly what is wrong with an animal. They need to be tactful and sympathetic so they can understand why owners feel upset when their pets are ill.

Observation
Good observational skills are important. This means being able to notice anything unusual however small. An animal can't say what is wrong and it's up to the vet to pick up on anything that is even slightly different.

Dexterity
Vets need to be good with their hands, so they can carry out examinations and treatments, while hurting the animals as little as possible. Treating small animals such as mice and hamsters can be very difficult.

This vet needs good observational skills to try and find out what is wrong with this dog through touching it.

Unsqueamish
Some jobs carried out by vets are messy and unpleasant, so vets need to have strong stomachs, and not be upset by blood and mess.

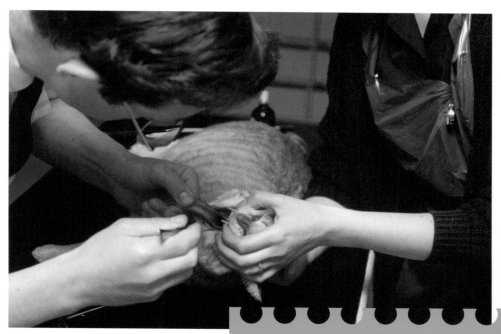

Performing an operation on a small animal such as a cat means you have to be good with your hands.

Organization

Keeping up-to-date records is important. Vets need to be able to express themselves clearly in writing. Most vets are **self-employed** which means they run their own business. To do this properly they need to be well organised and to keep up to date with a lot of paperwork.

fact file

There are only six universities in the UK which train vets. It takes at least five years to train and during this time students have to spend most holidays getting work experience with different types of animals.

Commitment

The job is tough and vets have to be prepared to work hard and long hours.

A day in the life of a vet

Mania Spalding

Mania is a vet in a practice with four branches, six vets and 20 nurses.

8.30 am   I arrive at the surgery and check emergencies that have been brought in and the animals which have been in the hospital overnight.

9.00 am   Consultation time, when I see sick animals brought in by owners. The usual time with each animal is ten minutes.

11.00 am   I help out in the operating theatre, check any new emergencies and if there's time make phone calls, do some paperwork and check blood test results.

1.00 pm   I try to take a proper lunch break, but don't always manage it.

2.00 pm   The afternoon consultation time begins.

3.00 pm   I go off to visit the large animals that can't be brought into the surgery. If there's time I fit in more paperwork. A growing number of people insure their pets against illness, which is sensible, but means a lot of insurance claim forms for us to fill in.

4.30 pm   Evening consultation time starts.

7.00 pm   The phone is switched on to the emergency system and if I'm not on night duty I clear up.

7.45 pm   With luck I'm on my way home. One in six nights I'm on night duty. In some practices vets are on call one night in two! Our night vet covers an area within 32 kilometres of the practice.

Sometimes I give advice over the phone. Owners are alarmed when a pet is ill, so I have to calm them down.

No matter how busy the night, the next day it's back into work at 8.30 am!

Large animals such as sheep and cows cannot be brought into the surgery so vets have to visit nearby farms such as this one.

Ten minutes are spent finding out what is wrong with this dog.

weblinks

For more information on training to be a vet, go to
www.waylinks.co.uk/
series/soyouwant/animals

Veterinary Nurse

What is a veterinary nurse?

Veterinary nurses work with vets caring for and treating different types of animals. They usually work in **private practices** but there are also opportunities for veterinary nurses to work in **laboratories**, **breeding stables** and zoos.

A veterinary nurse admits a sick animal booked in for treatment.

Veterinary nurses working in city practices deal mostly with domestic pets, such as cats, dogs, rabbits, canaries and budgerigars. Those working in country practices can find themselves driving out to farms to help with the treatment of farm stock.

Most veterinary nurses do a lot of different jobs. These include:

- admitting animals for treatment;
- preparing animals for the operating theatre;
- controlling the **anaesthetics** which keep an animal asleep during an operation;
- looking after animals recovering from surgery;
- keeping operating theatres and equipment clean and ready for use;

All kinds of animals

There are opportunities for veterinary nurses to work with unusual and exotic animals in zoos and wildlife parks. They also care for sick and abandoned animals in sanctuaries and shelters. Some specialise in the care of injured wild animals that need treatment before being returned to the wild.

- taking x-rays of patients;
- carrying out blood tests and sending them to laboratories;
- doing paperwork, ordering drugs and materials needed by the practice;
- talking to pet owners about treatment and how they should look after their pets when they return home.

Some veterinary nurses visit animals in their own homes or on farms, but they are much more likely to do their work in the veterinary practice.

The veterinary nurse is on hand to assist the vet during an operation.

Veterinary nurses have a lot of responsibility and do a much wider range of jobs than a nurse in a hospital working with humans.

Most veterinary practices carry out operations on animals. Veterinary nurses prepare animals for surgery by:

- checking that they are in good health and fit for the operation;
- giving them pre-meds or injections to sedate them and make them drowsy before they are given the anaesthetic which sends them to sleep.

A pre-med injection makes an animal calm and sleepy before it is given an anaesthetic.

Once vets have set up the anaesthetic, veterinary nurses take over and administer it in the correct amount throughout the operation.

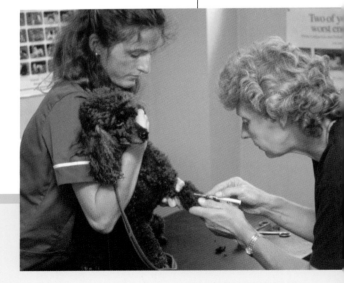

Good points and bad points

'As a veterinary nurse I love using my skills to make a sick animal better. It makes me feel I really can make a difference.'

'What I don't like is when pet owners decide not to follow my recommendations for certain treatments.'

The operating theatre must be prepared and ready for vets to carry out surgery.

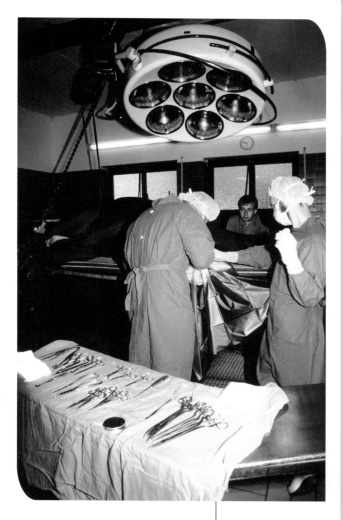

Afterwards, veterinary nurses check the animals as they recover from surgery. In some cases animals remain in the veterinary practice over night until they have made a full recovery. It is the responsibility of the veterinary nurses to make sure these animals are fed, watered and exercised. They also take blood tests and put in **feeding tubes** and take temperatures.

As well as caring for animals, veterinary nurses do quite a lot of administrative tasks and paperwork, sending samples off to laboratories to be tested, checking the results, checking medicine and equipment levels, and ordering new supplies.

Many practices have trainee veterinary nurses, and qualified veterinary nurses are often involved in their training, showing them how to do certain jobs and making sure they can do them properly.

Skills needed to be a veterinary nurse

Scientific
Veterinary nurses need to be interested in science, especially biology. They need to understand **medical terminology**.

Compassion
Veterinary nurses need to care about animals and be concerned about their health and welfare. However, they also need to be realistic about the job, as although they need to give all their patients the best care possible, they must be prepared for some patients to die and others to be **put down** because they are ill or in pain.

Tactful
Pet owners may be distressed when they bring in sick or injured animals. They need to be dealt with quietly and with understanding.

Learning on the job is an important part of training.

Calm and patient
Sick animals are not easy to handle and have to be treated very gently. It often takes time to carry out even simple tasks if an animal is in pain or frightened, so patience and a calm approach are important in this job.

Observation
Animals cannot say what is wrong, so veterinary nurses need to notice the very smallest changes in their appearance or behaviour.

Administration and paperwork have to be done.

Communication

Veterinary nurses need to keep clear, written records and follow spoken and written instructions from the vet carefully and accurately. They also have to explain to owners what treatment their pets have been given and what care they will need at home.

Teamwork

Veterinary nurses work closely with vets, other nurses, carers and pet owners.

Computer skills

Most practices use computers to record animal information, appointments, levels of medicine and stock and staff hours, so veterinary nurses need basic computer skills.

fact file

To train as a veterinary nurse you need five GCSEs at grade A-C including English language and a science subject or maths. Training takes place in a veterinary practice and at college. It is also possible to take a degree in veterinary nursing.

weblinks

For more information about the qualifications needed for veterinary nursing, go to
www.waylinks.co.uk/
series/soyouwant/animals

A day in the life of a veterinary nurse

Sarina Davis

Sarina is senior nurse in a veterinary practice made up of five full-time vets and a part-timer, three qualified nurses, two trainee nurses and two assistants.

9.15 am   I arrive at work and check that the animals due for surgery have been admitted and are ready for their pre-meds. I then look at our **in-patients** which have spent the night in the practice and deal with any problems.

10.15 am   I spend some time on administration, working out **duty rotas**, setting up college courses for trainee nurses. I also order new products and equipment for the practice.

11.15 am   Vets carry out operations until around 2.00 pm and I take my turn to assist them in the operating theatre. I check **anaesthetic** levels and keep the animals **anaesthetised**. I put in **drips** for fluids and **gastric tubes** so they can be fed. I also take x-rays.

2.00 pm   Surgery has finished and I go over to the kennel area to check on the animals that are recovering from operations. In this area it's general nursing care they need, to make sure all goes well and they make a good recovery.

3.30 pm   I organise a training session for the trainee nurses. They have to work and train in a practice before going to college to become qualified nurses.

4.30 pm   Owners will soon be arriving to collect their pets. We try to arrange for the nurse who was present during surgery to talk to the owners. I hand over pets and give advice to their owners on looking after them during the recovery period.

5.30 pm   One last check on the in-patients before setting off for home.

After advice from the nurse on looking after their pets, owners can take them home.

Patients need regular checks after they have had surgery.

weblinks

For a photo diary of another veterinary nurse, go to www.waylinks.co.uk/ series/soyouwant/animals

Zoo Keeper

What is a zoo keeper?

A zoo keeper is responsible for the health and care of the animals in a zoo and also for the safety of visitors. Zoos are to be found in towns and cities and in the country. There are also wildlife parks where the animals roam across large areas.

Some zoos are very large with many animals, others are smaller and may specialize in a particular type of animal, for example, monkeys or reptiles. Other zoos have collections of animals from a particular area of the world such as South America or Asia.

Zoo keepers can either work with different animals or specialize in caring for a particular type of animal.

Zoo keepers are responsible for the daily care of the animals.

So you want to work with animals?

A home from home

Environmental enrichment is becoming more and more important in zoos. This means making the animals' living conditions as similar to their natural habitat as possible, so they keep active and busy.

Ways of keeping the animals active include moving their feeding areas, changing the times at which they are fed and adding interest to their **enclosures** by putting in new plants, trees and stones or rocks.

Today zoos are not just places where visitors come to look at animals.

Visitors have plenty of questions to ask.

- They aim to teach people about different species or types of animals, where they come from, and how they live in the wild.
- They are involved in **conservation programmes**, protecting **endangered species** which are in danger of dying out, and encouraging them to breed.

Zoo keepers play an important part in these activities.

Many people want to work in zoos, so finding a job is not easy. Sometimes people work in zoos as volunteers in their spare time, to learn about the work and to show how much they want the job.

weblinks

For more information on a zoo, go to www.waylinks.co.uk/ series/soyouwant/animals

Whatever the type or size of the zoo, the keepers working in them have similar responsibilities.

Feeding the animals
In order to stay healthy, animals need to eat food that is similar to the food they would eat in the wild. This can mean a lot of preparation, chopping vegetables and adding vitamins and **supplements**.

Zoo keepers have to ensure that everything is clean and tidy.

Some creatures such as mink and weasels have a natural diet of smaller animals, and zoo keepers have to feed them dead rats and mice, or live insects such as locusts or mealworms.

Checking health and well being
Zoo keepers see the animals every day, so they are the people most likely to notice if something is wrong. They keep daily written records on what an animal eats and how they are behaving, whether they are lying quietly in a corner, or are being lively and sociable.

Good points and bad points

'The best thing about the job is getting to know the animals so well, building things in their cages and thinking of ideas to make them think and move and keep active.'

'The worst job is mucking out the **drain buckets** and clearing the **sludge** that has gathered there.'

If an animal is ill, the zoo keeper will help the vet to catch it and examine it. Zoo animals are very different from domestic pets. They are not used to being handled and are nervous of human contact, so treating them when they are ill is not easy.

Mucking out and cleaning cages and pens

Cleanliness is vital, so zoo keepers spend a lot of time cleaning and scrubbing out.

Visitor and animal safety

Most visitors are well behaved, but some are tempted to feed the animals. Ice creams and chocolate are fine for humans, but can make animals ill. Zoo keepers have to look out for food being dropped or pushed into enclosures.

Sometimes visitors try to push their fingers through the barrier to stroke the animals. This is very dangerous and zoo keepers have to be on the lookout for such behaviour. Zoo keepers also check that barriers, fences and notices are in place, carry out security checks and lock up after closing time.

weblinks

For a factsheet, game and photo diary of a zoo keeper, go to
www.waylinks.co.uk/
series/soyouwant/animals

Skills needed to be a zoo keeper

Knowledgeable
Zoo keepers need to be knowledgeable about the animals in their zoo and have a real interest in the animals they look after. This includes knowing about the countries the animals come from, and how they live in the wild, as well as their habits and behaviour.

Physically fit
This job is physically demanding, so zoo keepers have to be fit and strong, able to lift and stretch and bend easily, pick up heavy sacks of feed and bedding, and be happy working outside whatever the weather.

Noting details of an animal's appetite and behaviour is part of the job.

Observation
Being observant and learning about the habits and behaviour of both individuals and groups of animals is important in order to notice changes, even very small ones. A slight change in an animal's behaviour can be a sign that something might be wrong with the animal.

Communication
An important part of the job is communication with visitors to the zoo. Keepers have to be able to explain things simply and in an interesting way to visitors and answer their questions.

Keepers working in animal parks need to cover a lot of ground.

First aid

Zoo keepers are often the first people to discover sick or injured animals and they need to know how to look after them until the vet arrives.

Responsible

Zoo keepers need to be sensible and responsible, as working with wild animals can be dangerous. They always need to be aware of the safety of the animals, the visitors and themselves, because one careless moment can lead to tragedy.

fact file

There are no set qualifications to become a zoo keeper. Most zoos want people with GCSEs, while others ask for A-levels. Some large zoos look for a degree in a subject like animal science. Others want people who have worked with animals in stables, kennels or animal shelters. There is a zoo animal management course, which many zoo keepers take.

A day in the life of a zoo keeper

Oliver Walter

Oliver worked as a volunteer at a zoo, before becoming a zoo keeper.

8.00 am   I work in the small mammal section, with animals from South America including **marmosets, tamarins** and **anteaters**.

There are two animal houses, one for **diurnal animals** which wake in the daytime and the other for **nocturnal animals** which sleep during the day.

The nocturnal house has lights dimmed during the day so the animals wake up. During the night the lights shine brightly and the animals sleep.

I quickly check the animals, then attend the briefing session where morning jobs are given out.

9.00 am   I have a section of a house to work in. I check each cage to make sure food has been eaten, the animals look well and are behaving normally.

I change the water, clean the dishes, check temperature and **humidity** levels and scatter food, hiding live crickets around the cage so the animals can hunt for them.

11.00 am   Soiled areas of cages are cleaned daily. When an animal is **relocated** the empty cage is thoroughly scrubbed.

Relocation could be for a number of reasons, such as the need to re-structure a family group because infants are being pushed out by adults, or because animals are being moved to a different zoo.

2.00 pm A briefing session to sort out afternoon schedules.

All the animals are fed in the afternoon. Those needing medicine are given it in their food, perhaps in a banana, or a honey sandwich.

4.00 pm I give a keeper's talk for visitors and then answer questions.

5.00 pm A last look around before going home.

A keeper's talk.

Feeding an anteater.

Glossary

allergy – reaction in the body to something such as food or pollen.

anaesthetic – substance that causes unconsciousness for a short time.

anaesthetise – to give an anaesthetic to cause unconsciousness.

animal beautician – a person who makes animals look their best.

animal behaviourist – someone who tries to cure animals of bad habits such as barking or running away.

anteater – South American mammal that eats almost nothing but ants.

aquarium – a water tank in which fish and sea animals are kept.

artificial reef – a man-made ridge of rock or sand lying just beneath the sea.

bookkeeping – writing down details of business actions, such as what has been bought and sold.

breaking in – training a horse so it is ready to be ridden.

breed standards – the qualities required in a particular strain or group of animals. For example, a prize-winning poodle will have a certain shape of face and body.

breeding programmes – projects to encourage animals or birds to have babies.

breeding stable – a horse centre where particular stallions and mares are encouraged to breed.

bridle – headgear for controlling a horse.

conservation programme – protection and management of the environment.

cross country riding – horse riding across fields and woods and away from roads.

diet instructions – information on eating the right food.

diurnal animals – creatures that wake up during the day.

drain buckets – containers placed to catch dirty water.

drip – a piece of medical equipment used to put liquid into a vein.

duty rota – list of jobs and who is to do them.

ecosystems – the relationship between animals and plants and the way they live together.

enclosure – a fenced-in area.

endangered species – a type of animal whose numbers have become so small that it is likely to become extinct or die out.

endurance rider – horses and their mounts travelling long distances often in remote areas over several days.

environmental enrichment – making the homes of zoo animals more interesting so they do not become bored.

estuaries – the area of river where it grows wider before flowing into the sea.

feeding tube – a length of flexible piping inserted into a person or animal, through which food is passed. It is used to ensure those who are unconscious or too ill to eat normally receive the substances they need.

fish farms – places where fish and shellfish are bred and kept in large tanks or enclosures until they reach the right size to be sold as food.

foot and mouth disease – an illness affecting animals with cloven hooves such as cows and sheep.

gastric tube – piping fed through the mouth down into the stomach.

grooming table – equipment used by animal beauticians and groomers, which positions animals at the correct level for treatment.

head collar – band of leather or rope placed round an animal's head.

health programme – a list of activities including diet and exercise, aimed at keeping an animal or person fit and well.

holding unit – section of a shelter where animals are kept for health checks upon their arrival.

homing unit – section of a shelter housing animals which are ready to go to new owners.

humidity – level of moisture in the air.

in-patient – a person who is staying in hospital for treatment; an animal staying at a vet's surgery.

invertebrates – animals that do not have backbones.

isolation unit – place where people or animals are kept apart from others, while they are checked for diseases.

laboratories – room equipped for scientific experiments.

litter tray – a shallow open box filled with earth or material which animals use as a toilet.

maltreated – to be hurt or neglected.

marine mammals – animals that suckle their young and live in the sea.

marmoset – small tree-dwelling monkey from South America.

medical terminology – words used by doctors to describe conditions, treatment and equipment.

mites – tiny creatures, many of them live by burrowing into the skin of humans and animals.

modern apprentice – young people training to do a job.

mongoose – small long-tailed animal, that kills snakes.

neutered – removal of an animal's sexual (reproductive) organs.

nocturnal animals – creatures that wake up at night.

outlets – openings.

parasite – creature that lives on other animals.

pre-med – a drink or injection given before an operation to calm a person or animal before they are given an anaesthetic.

private practice – a situation where working professional people such as vets and doctors are self-employed and charge patients or organisations for the work they do for them.

put down – to kill an animal because it is very old or in pain.

rehome – find a new family for an animal.

relocate – move to another place.

research ship – a vessel which travels the seas collecting specimens and carrying out investigations.

restraint – equipment to keep an animal still.

saddle – leather seat strapped on to a horse's back.

scaling – removing material that has built up on and around teeth.

sedate – give medication to calm a person or animal.

self-employed – working for yourself, organising your business and keeping business details.

sludge – mud or sewage.

specimen – an example of an animal or plant.

supplements – extra items such as vitamins or minerals added to a diet to keep a person or animal healthy.

tamarin – a small squirrel monkey.

temperate – warm, not too hot and not too cold.

valves – attachments on pipes or tubes which control the flow of liquid or gas.

working pupil – a young person who trains on the job while being employed by an organisation.

Further Information

So do you still want to work with animals?

This book cannot hope to cover all the jobs that involve working with animals. There are many others, including kennel worker, stable groom and dog handler which are not mentioned here. But the book does try to give you an idea of what working with animals is like.

Reading it you will have discovered that working with animals often means long hours – getting up early and staying late, sometimes working over weekends and bank holidays, and being outside in all weathers.

Working with animals brings its own rewards, such as playing a real part in caring for different creatures and helping to make sure they are healthy and well looked after, or encouraging other people to learn more about the animal world.

The only way to know for certain that a career is right for you is to find out for yourself what it involves. Read as much as you can on the subject and talk to people you know who work with animals.

If you are at secondary school and seriously interested in a certain career, ask your careers teacher if he or she could arrange for some work experience. This means spending some time, usually a week, in an area of your chosen profession. In this instance, you could ask for work at a zoo, a riding school, an animal shelter, a veterinary practice or an aquarium, watching what goes on and how the people working there spend their time.

Books

If you want to find out more about working with animals, you will find the following helpful:

Careers Working with Animals, by Allan Shepherd, published by Kogan Page, 2002.

Working in Outdoor Jobs, published by Connexions, 2002.

Working in Work with Animals, published by Connexions 2002.

BHS Guide to Careers with Horses, published by the British Horse Society, 2001.

weblinks

For websites relevant to this book, go to www.waylinks.co.uk/series/soyouwant/animals

Useful addresses

Animal Groomer

Pet Care Trust
Bedford Business Centre
170 Mile Road
Bedford, MK42 9TW
Tel: 01234 273933

Animal Shelter Worker

Animal Care College
Ascot House
High Street
Ascot
Berkshire, SL5 7JG
Tel: 01344 628269

College of Animal Welfare
London Road
Godmanchester
Cambridgeshire, PE29 2LJ
Tel: 01480 831177

Lantra Trust
Lantra House
National Agricultural Centre
Kenilworth
Warwickshire, CV8 2LG
Tel: 024 7669 6996

Marine Biologist

Southampton Oceanography
Centre
University of Southampton
Waterfront Campus
European Way
Southampton, SO14 3ZH
Tel: 023 8059 6666

Natural Environment
Research Council
Polaris House
North Star Avenue
Swindon, SN2 1EU
Tel: 01793 411500

Society for Underwater
Technology
80 Coleman Street
London, EC2R 5BJ
Tel: 0207 382 2601

Riding Instructor

Association of British Riding
Schools
Queen's Chambers
38-40 Queen Street
Penzance
Cornwall, TR18 4BH
Tel: 01736 369440

British Horse Society
Stoneleigh Deer Park
Kenilworth
Warwickshire, CV8 2XZ
Tel: 01926 707700 / 08701
202244

Riding for the Disabled
Association
Lavinia Norfolk House
Avenue R
National Agricultural Centre
Stoneleigh Park
Kenilworth
Warwickshire, CV8 2LY
Tel: 024 7669 6510

Veterinary Surgeon

The British Veterinary
Association
7 Mansfield Street
London, W1G 9NQ
Tel: 0207 636 6541

The Royal College of
Veterinary Surgeons
Belgravia House
62-64 Horseferry Road
London, SW1P 2AF
Tel: 0207 222 2001

Veterinary Nurse

The British Veterinary
Nursing Association
11 Shenval House
South Road
Harlow
Essex, CM20 2BD
Tel: 01279 450567

Zoo Keeper

Association of British Wild
Animal Keepers
David Fowler
Cotswold Wildlife Park
Burford
Oxfordshire, OX18 4JW
Tel: 01993 823006

Federation of Zoos
Regents Park
London, NW1 4RY
Tel: 0207 586 0230

Volunteers Co-ordinator
Forum
Bristol Zoo Gardens
Clifton
Bristol, BS8 3HA
Tel: 0117 970 6176

Index